9 TO THRIVE

SIDE HUSTLE TO SUCCESS

Izu Nwachukwu

IZU NWACHUKWU
1st Edition

Publication Date: October 2024
Price: ₹ 499 $ 2.99
ISBN: *978-93-5847-517-3*
Published by:
Adhyyan Books
Office No. 125,
Opposite Vivanta by Taj,
DDA SFS. Pocket-1, Dwarka,
Sec-22, New Delhi-110077
Website: http://adhyyanbooks.com
E-mail: contact@adhyyanbooks.com

Printed at: Repro Printers, Delhi

Contents

1

INTRODUCTION

Why Become a Side Hustler?

In today's rapidly changing world, the way we work has undergone a seismic shift, largely driven by the global pandemic, COVID-19. As our homes transformed into offices, and our living rooms became virtual meeting spaces, we found ourselves with an unexpected commodity: time! The daily commute disappeared, and for many, the concept of a "nine-to-five" job took on new meaning.

However, this newfound flexibility also highlighted the vulnerability of traditional employment. Jobs that once seemed stable suddenly vanished, many were laid off leaving countless individuals without their primary source of income. It was a stark reminder that relying solely on one income stream might not be the safest path forward.

Enter the side hustle, a concept that gained immense popularity during these changing times. It's not a replacement for your full-time job, nor is it quite the same as starting a business from scratch. Instead, think of it as an adaptable middle ground—a way to earn extra income while maintaining your regular employment.

So, why should you consider embracing the side hustle? Well, the motivations are different. Some embark on this journey to supplement their income, providing a financial cushion that can ease the pressure of bills and expenses. Others are driven by a desire for change, a longing for something different from their routine and unsatisfactory job. Many see the side hustle as a chance for personal and professional growth, a platform to explore their creative passions, or a pathway to becoming their own boss eventually. And in the era of economic uncertainty, having a side hustle can serve as a vital financial safety net.

Is Your Job a Good Business Partner?

If you're currently employed full-time but dream of becoming an entrepreneur without immediately sacrificing your reliable paycheck, consider this: Your job can play a more significant role in your side hustle journey. Think of it as a business partner or an investor in your side hustle venture. It's the source of your steady income, and you can allocate a portion of that income into your side hustle as a long-term investment until your hustle starts paying dividends.

However, here's a crucial takeaway point: Your job should not be an all-consuming presence. To successfully manage your side hustle alongside your regular job, you need the time and energy to devote to both. Your workweek should conclude at a reasonable hour, and your workdays should not spill into the weekends, and you must be disciplined about this! Achieving this balance is essential for your overall well-being and the success of your side hustle.

Allow me to share a personal story that underscores the importance of balance. For years, I toiled in a demanding job that required late nights and weekend work, the pressure of deadlines and continuous sales pitches meant I sometimes worked up to 16 hours per day, 6 days a week. By the time I returned home, I lacked the mental and physical energy to focus on my side hustle, and a ton of anxiety about my performance at work. The result? A stalled side hustle, and Burnout!

So, if your job leaves you with little time or energy for your side hustle, it's bound to be an uphill battle.

If you're not quite ready to take the leap into full-time entrepreneurship, look for a job that allows you enough time and financial stability to invest in your side hustle. Your job should be a supportive partner, one that gives you the time and relative freedom to invest in your entrepreneurial aspirations and respects your need for a work-life balance.

In the chapters ahead, I'll guide you through the process of launching and nurturing your side hustle. I'll help you discover the formula to finding your ideal side hustle idea, create a robust plan, and manage your time efficiently. I'll delve into the nitty-gritty of handling your finances, building valuable networks, and conquering the common challenges faced by side hustlers.

Be SMART! Setting Goals for Your Side Hustle Journey

What do you want to achieve with your side hustle? Are you just looking for extra income, aiming to move into self-employment, or do you have broader, more ambitious objectives in mind?

Setting clear and specific goals is not just a good idea; it's a crucial step in your journey toward side hustling success. These goals will serve as your North Star, guiding your decisions, helping you manage your time effectively, and keeping you motivated even when faced with daunting obstacles and challenges.

In "9 to Thrive: Side Hustle to Success," we're not just going to talk about the importance of goals; I am going to provide you with the tools and insights you need to set and achieve them. So, let's embark on this section with the aim of not only understanding the significance of setting goals but also equipping you with the knowledge and strategies to make your side hustle aspirations a reality.

The Power of Clear Goals

You're on a road trip with no map, no GPS, and no destination in mind. You're just driving aimlessly, hoping you'll eventually stumble upon something interesting. While this might sound like an adventurous way to spend an afternoon, it's hardly a practical approach when it comes to your side hustle.

Goals are the roadmap of your side hustle journey. They provide direction, purpose, and a sense of accomplishment along the way. Without them, you risk drifting aimlessly, making arbitrary decisions, and feeling overwhelmed by the sheer number of possibilities, not to mention your day job. Without measurable goals to hold yourself accountable, you can easily slip back into the comfort zone or familiarity that your 9-5 provides, and just like that your hustle sits in limbo!

When you set clear goals for your side hustle, you're essentially defining your destination. Whether that destination is to generate a specific amount of income, transition into full-time entrepreneurship, or gain a certain level of recognition in your field, your goals give you a target to aim for. They transform your side hustle from a vague idea into a structured plan and bring it to life.

The Different Dimensions of Side Hustle Goals

Side hustle goals can take various forms, depending on your aspirations and where you are in your journey. Here are some common dimensions of side hustle goals:

Financial Goals: These are perhaps the most tangible and immediate. You might set financial goals like earning an extra $1,000 per month from your side hustle, saving a specific amount for a major purchase, or paying off certain debts or investing the money for financial gain. Financial goals provide you with a clear measure of success and can be excellent motivators.

Professional Goals: If you're looking to transition from your full-time job to self-employment or advance in your chosen field, professional goals are crucial. They could include securing a certain number of clients, completing a certification, or building a portfolio of successful projects.

Personal Development Goals: Side hustles aren't just about money; they're about personal growth too. You might set goals related to acquiring new skills, expanding your network, or challenging yourself creatively. These goals contribute to your overall development and can lead to a more fulfilling life.

Time Management Goals: Efficiently managing your time is often a significant challenge for side hustlers. Setting goals related to time management can help you strike the right balance between your full-time job, your side hustle, and your personal life. For example, you might set a goal to dedicate a certain number of hours each week to your side hustle.

Networking and Relationship Goals: Building a supportive network can be instrumental to side hustle success. Consider setting goals related to expanding your network, collaborating with others in your industry, or attending a certain number of networking events or workshops.

Creativity and Innovation Goals: If your side hustle involves a creative endeavor, such as writing, design, or art, you might set goals to produce a certain number of pieces, launch a creative project, or experiment with new styles and techniques.

Remember, your side hustle journey is unique to you, and so are your goals. It's essential to align your goals with your personal aspirations and circumstances. What might be a significant financial goal for one person may not hold the same importance for another. Your goals should reflect what matters most to you and what you hope to achieve with your side hustle.

The SMART Approach to Goal Setting

Setting goals is not merely about jotting down desires; it involves a structured approach to ensure that your goals are achievable and actionable. One effective method for goal setting is the SMART framework. SMART stands for **Specific**, **Measurable, Achievable, Relevant**, and **Time-bound**. Let's break down each aspect:

Specific: Your goal should be clear and unambiguous. Instead of a vague goal like "earn more money," make it specific by saying, "earn an additional $1,000 per month through my side hustle."

Measurable: You should be able to quantify your goal, so you know when you've achieved it. In the example above, the measurement is clear: $1000 per month.

Achievable: While it's great to aim high, your goal should be attainable given your current resources and circumstances. Setting unrealistic goals can lead to frustration, demotivation and burnout. Ask yourself if your goal is within reach with the effort and resources you can realistically allocate.

Relevant: Your goal should be aligned with your overall objectives. Ensure that it's relevant to your side hustle and contributes to your long-term vision. If you're aiming to become a freelance writer, setting a goal to learn web development might not be directly relevant.

Time-bound: Finally, set a timeframe for achieving your goal. Having a deadline creates a sense of urgency and helps you stay focused. For instance, you might set a goal to earn that extra $1000 per month within six months.

Let's look at an example of a SMART goal for a side hustle:

"I will earn an additional $1000 per month through my side hustle by securing three new clients for my freelance graphic design services within the next six months."

This goal is specific (earn $1000 per month), measurable (through securing three clients), achievable (given the freelancer's skills and the demand for graphic design), relevant (aligned with the graphic design side hustle), and time-bound (within the next six months).

Using the SMART framework for your side hustle goals offers several advantages:

Clarity: SMART goals provide crystal-clear direction. You know exactly what you're working toward, which reduces confusion and decision-making fatigue (yes, it's a real thing).

Motivation: Achieving SMART goals can be highly motivating. As you make progress and reach milestones, you'll experience a sense of accomplishment that fuels your drive to continue.

Focus: SMART goals keep you focused on what truly matters. When you have a set of well-defined goals, you can filter out distractions and prioritize tasks that contribute directly to your objectives.

Measurement: You can track your progress easily with SMART goals. You'll know when you're on track, when you need to adjust your efforts, and when you've successfully achieved a goal.

Accountability: SMART goals hold you accountable. When you commit to specific, measurable targets with deadlines, you're more likely to stay committed and complete the necessary actions.

Adaptability: If you find that a goal isn't working as intended, the SMART framework allows you to adjust and refine your goals to better suit your evolving circumstances.

Now, with an understanding of the importance of setting goals and the SMART framework, it's time to apply this knowledge to your side hustle journey. In the upcoming chapters, we'll delve deeper into various types of goals, explore strategies to stay motivated, and provide practical exercises to help you set and achieve your own SMART goals.

Your side hustle journey is a dynamic and exciting path filled with opportunities for growth and success. By setting clear, actionable goals, you're already taking a significant step toward making your side hustle dreams a reality.

Before we conclude this chapter, take a moment to reflect on your own side hustle aspirations. What are your primary motivations for starting a side hustle? What do you hope to achieve, both personally and professionally? What challenges do you anticipate along the way?

Start outlining your own SMART goals for your side hustle. Consider your current circumstances, available resources, and the timeframe that makes the most sense for you. Write down your goals, ensuring they are Specific, Measurable, Achievable, Relevant, and Time-bound.

Remember, your goals are unique to your journey, so make them meaningful and inspiring to you. As you continue reading "9 to Thrive: Side Hustle to Success" you'll gain more insights and strategies to help you turn these goals into remarkable achievements.

Reflections

• Is your current job a good fit, is it a good business partner and side hustle friendly?

• What are your goals for a side hustle, are they clearly defined and realistic?

• Are you working SMART, can you apply the SMART framework to your side hustle ambitions?

2

UNLOCKING YOUR INNER ENTREPRENEUR

Where Do You Even Begin?

Welcome to the thrilling part of your side hustle journey – finding the side hustle idea that will be your guiding star in this entrepreneurial galaxy.

There are so many ideas out there, and with so many Tik Tok gurus and internet sensation touting all sorts of ideas as the next big thing from NFTs to fidget spinners as the next "get rich quick" opportunity, it can be quite daunting, confusing, and even scary in terms of choosing a business idea.

You might be thinking, "How do I even begin?" Don't worry; I've got your back! In this chapter I'll share a simple directional framework or formula that can be used as a guide to your choosing your first, second or third side hustle.

Identifying Your Passions and Skills

Here's the thing: Your side hustle doesn't have to be just about making money; it can also be about making your heart sing. Start by listing your passions and skills, those things that get you out of bed even before your alarm clock dares to beep.

But there must be a market or demand for it, otherwise, you'll be pouring money into a hobby and may see little returns! So, there are two approaches I can suggest:

Products: Here you are taking a product to market, it could be something new and innovative or something already in the market and in high demand.

The latter means you'll spend less time and money in terms of researching and developing your own products, however developing your own products can give you and edge and exclusivity in the market especially if there is a need for the product.

Skills & Services: These are skills that you already possess, possibly from years of experience in your current job or you've built up along the years and you are good at.

Your skills are secret weapons here and don't underestimate the ability to draw in an income stream by using them.

A great example is a lady who I know, she had been a corporate personal assistant for years, but she had just as much experience in fitness for years. She became certified as a personal trainer and took on clients in the evenings and weekends at their homes or open spaces, which eventually led to her opening her own indoor gym, while holding down her day job!

The Magic of Alignment

The magic happens when your passions, skills, or product and market demand intertwine. That's where the sweet spot of your side hustle idea lies, and there is nothing that says you can't offer both Product and Skills & Services as multiple side hustles. So, think about it, and you've got yourself a potential side hustle.

But how do you ensure that your passions align with a market need? It's about finding that perfect balance, like matching pieces of a puzzle. Here's how to make the magic of alignment work for you:

Passion-Driven Market Research: Once you've identified your passions and skills, dive into market research. Explore whether there's a demand for products or services related to your passions.

Solve Your Audience's Problems: Think about how your passions can solve problems or fulfill needs in the market. Who is your target audience and how can your side hustle solve their problems, where no one else has.

Unique Selling Proposition (USP): Determine what makes your side hustle unique. Your passion can be a powerful USP that sets you apart from competitors.

Scalability: Consider whether your passion allows for scalability. While you may start small, can you envision your side hustle growing over time?

Testing the Waters: Sometimes, the best way to see if your passion aligns with the market is to dip your toes in. Offer your product or service on a small scale to gauge interest and demand.

Customer Feedback: Pay attention to what potential customers are saying. Their feedback can guide your direction and help you refine your offering.

The Formula to Find Your Side Hustle

But before you declare yourself the next business tycoon, it's time to do a bit of detective work. Research, my dear side hustler, is your best friend. What's the demand for your side hustle idea? Who are your potential customers, and where do they hang out? Is there competition, and if so, how can you stand out like a neon sign in a power outage?

I give you the side hustle formula:

Product or Service + Market Demand x Job Agreeability - Risk = Side Hustle Sweet Spot.

Product, Skills & Services: As mentioned, this refers to your passions, skills, and products you want to bring to market as a side hustler.

Market Demand: If your skills or products are in demand, or if you carve out a niche market that isn't heavily competitive, this will increase your chance of success.

Job Agreeability: This factor relates to your first business partner, your day job. Does it afford you the time, energy, and finances to invest into your side hustle. The higher your full-time job agreeability the more likely you will have the time, energy and finances to start your hustle.

Risk: Consider the risks associated with your side hustle idea. Some ventures come with higher risks, like substantial upfront investment, while others have lower risks, such as starting with minimal capital. Minimizing risk is often a smart approach, especially if you're new to entrepreneurship.

By assessing these factors, you can refine your side hustle idea further and align it with your preferences and goals.

Below are examples of side hustles that often align well with the side hustle formula:

Drop shipping: This is a product-focused side hustle. You can create an e-commerce store and sell products directly to customers without holding any inventory, the website works 24 hours a day and you invest in marketing or use third party platforms like Amazon. The key is to find unique or trending products that have high demand.

Freelance Writing: If you have strong writing skills, offering freelance writing services can be a lucrative side hustle. Many businesses and websites require quality content. And you can do this in your free time or weekends.

Graphic Design Services: Graphic designers can offer their skills to create logos, marketing materials, and graphics for businesses and individuals.

Virtual Assistance: Utilize your organizational and administrative skills to become a virtual assistant for businesses or entrepreneurs who need help with tasks like email management, scheduling, and more, this can be done remotely.

Fitness Coaching: If you have a passion for fitness, become a certified fitness coach and offer personal training services. You can even create online workout programs.

Handmade Crafts: If you're skilled at crafting, consider selling handmade crafts on platforms like Etsy. Unique and personalized items often do well.

Content Creation on YouTube or Podcasting: If you have expertise or a passion for a specific topic, consider creating content on YouTube or starting a podcast. You can earn from ads and sponsorships.

These examples demonstrate that a side hustle can take various forms, from selling products online to offering services, but by no means an exhaustible list of what you can do.

The key takeout here is that businesses that can function almost on autopilot or can be modelled around your free time, such as online businesses or remote working skills tend to easily align well with side hustling.

Reflections

- What passions or skills are you considering for your side hustle?
- Will you be selling a product, or your skill set?

- Is your side hustle aligned with the marketplace, is it in demand does it solve a problem for your audience?

- Does the side hustle formula validate your side hustle?

3

PLANNING YOUR SIDE HUSTLE

What's In a Plan?

This chapter is all about planning your side hustle for success. In the previous chapters, we've explored how to identify your passions, skills, and potential side hustle ideas. It's time to dive into the nitty-gritty details of turning your side hustle dreams into a well-executed plan.

Finding Your Target Audience

To truly understand your audience, you must get inside their heads. What drives them? What problems do they face? What solutions are they seeking? With the answers to these questions, you can tailor your side hustle to meet their needs.

However, it's important to recognize that your audience isn't a monolith. Within your target demographic, there are distinct segments with unique preferences. It's crucial to identify these segments and customize your approach to resonate with each one.

Research plays a pivotal role here. Use surveys, market analysis, and feedback from potential customers to refine your understanding of your audience. This in-depth knowledge will guide your product or service offerings, marketing strategies, and communication style.

Now I clearly understand that you may not have the time nor the money to spend on creating your own market research, sending out surveys, organizing focus groups etc. So, you can look into using third party research that may already have insights into the audience you are aiming for, sometimes a simple Google search can be enough to give you the information you need.

Crafting a Solid Side Hustle Business Plan

A business plan is your roadmap to success. It outlines your goals, strategies, and action steps. A well-crafted plan not only serves as a guide but also demonstrates your commitment to potential investors or partners.

Your understanding of your audience will refine your business plan. Consider the following elements:

Mission Statement: Define the purpose and core values of your side hustle. How does it align with your audience's needs and desires?

Goals and Objectives: Set clear, achievable goals. These should be specific, measurable, and time-bound (SMART) as we highlighted in chapter 1.

Market Analysis: Provide a detailed analysis of your target market. Who are your potential customers, and what are their characteristics? What are the trends and opportunities in your industry?

Competitive Analysis: Identify your competitors and analyze their strengths and weaknesses. Is the market saturated or is it a niche with opportunities for a newcomer? How can you differentiate your side hustle in a crowded market, what is the unique value that you offer, that no one else offers?

Marketing Strategy: Based on your audience's preferences, outline your marketing plan. Will you focus on social media, content marketing, email campaigns, or a combination of different channels? How much will you invest into your marketing, define a clear monthly budget.

Operational Plan: Detail how your side hustle will operate day-to-day. Consider the resources, equipment, and technologies you'll need to deliver your product or service effectively, and what it will financially cost to run the hustle.

Expected Revenue: Based on your market research, target audience and competitiveness in the marketplace, outline your expected annual income from the side hustle and then break it down to a monthly or quarterly basis minus your operational costs. The monthly revenue breakdown should help you to see how you are performing and keep track of your profit.

Setting Realistic Expectations

Setting expectations is about being honest with yourself. It's exciting to envision the success of your side hustle and becoming financially independent overnight, but it's also essential to recognize the challenges and uncertainties ahead, and the importance of being realistic about the time and effort it can sometimes take to become a success.

Setting unrealistic or over ambitious expectations can work against you. As an example, if you expect your side hustle to generate an income of $10,000 p/m and $120,000 in your first year, but you only manage $1,000 p/m for 6 months, it's easy to see this as a failure and lose motivation or drive, and eventually abandon the side hustle.

Be honest with yourself, there is no such thing as an overnight success! it's a side hustle which you invest a few hours a day, and not every waking hour with the full weight of a venture capital investment in the hundreds of thousands of dollars. So, think of it as a child that needs the time and investment to grow into a full-on adult based on the ratio of time and monetary input you give it.

The Importance of Finding a Business Partner

I usually advise individuals who want to start up their business to consider taking on a business partner, as there are benefits to doing so, and the same can apply to a side hustle. The decision to have a business partner is significant. It can unlock synergy and enhance your side hustle potential. Here's why finding a business partner can be a valuable consideration:

Diverse Skillsets and Expertise: Partners bring diverse skills and expertise to your side hustle, forming a well-rounded team. Be sure to pick a partner that can contribute here, as someone who brings no discernible skills or value could see you doing most of the work, carrying them and the business all by yourself.

Complementary Networks: You've heard the saying "Your network is your net worth", Partners may have valuable connections that expand your reach and open doors to collaborations or new customers and clientele.

Shared Vision, Purpose and Drive: Choosing a partner that shares the same vision as you can help keep your motivation for the business going. If you pick a partner that doesn't necessarily believe in the vision, this could result in constant friction with your partner, for example if your focus for your side hustle is more about passion than making money, but your partner is all about the money, they may focus on diluting the purpose in order to drive more revenue, which can see both your expectations clashing.

Accountability and Motivation: Having the right partner is a great way to keep each other accountable and for the side hustle. Working on your own with a day job, family challenges and life in general can sometimes be overwhelming especially if burn out sets in. With a partner, you can set bi-weekly or monthly meetings as required to make sure you both stay on track and progress any assigned tasks and the side hustle.

Divide and Conquer: Partners can divide responsibilities for efficient scaling efforts. This means you don't have to do it all to get the side hustle off the ground, you can divide and conquer by sharing tasks between each other to lighten the workload. If it requires 20 crucial tasks to get the side hustle going with a partner you end up with 10 tasks, which gives you time back.

Reduce Financial Burden: With a partner, you don't need to foot the entire bill when it comes to funding your side hustle, especially if you are going down the route of selling a product, which requires investment for purchasing stock, storage, and sales channels etc. If the start-up cost is $20,000, you can equally split the cost based on your shares. This can see the financial burden on you reduced, allowing you to utilize your money elsewhere.

Remember that the decision to partner up should align with your side hustle's unique needs and your own preferences. If you choose to take on a partner, then selecting the right partner for your side hustle is important, it's just like selecting a partner for a relationship. If they aren't a right fit, you could end up focusing on your differences rather than the side hustle. Look for a partner who shares the same passion, vision, values, has a personality that doesn't clash with you and can bring skills that can add value.

Budgeting for Your Side Hustle

Effective budgeting is the backbone of a successful side hustle. Just like your business plan it ensures you're using your resources wisely and helps you achieve your financial goals. Here's how to create a budget for your side business:

Startup Costs: When considering startup costs, break them down into categories such as equipment, technology, marketing materials, inventory, business registration and legal fees. This way you can see how much initial investment is required against each line item, this can help you decide if a cost for a line item is crucial at the time, or if it can be postponed further down the line, saving you on the costs.

Operational Budget: Create a budget that aligns with your business's monthly needs. This budget should include all reoccurring costs required to keep your hustle operational. You can break this down as a monthly spend to clearly understand how much outgoings you should expect every month. As per your business plan, you can layer the operational costs with your forecasted income to see how profitable your side hustle is.

Risk-Adjusted Budget: Create a budget that accounts for potential challenges and risks specific to your audience or the marketplace This includes setting aside a portion of your budget as a financial cushion to weather unexpected downturns.

Conclusion

In this chapter, we've explored the importance of planning your side hustle meticulously. Your audience's preferences and needs should be at the core of your planning process. Crafting a solid business plan, setting realistic expectations, and budgeting wisely are essential steps.

Additionally, we've delved into the potential benefits of finding a business partner. While not necessary for all side hustles, a partner can provide shared workload, motivation, accountability, cost sharing, and risk mitigation.

As you move forward on your side hustle journey, remember that your audience is your compass. Keep their needs in focus, and you'll be well on your way to side hustle success.

Reflections

- Do you understand your audience's needs, do you have any market research to back up your claims?

- How does your side hustle reflect with your business plan, have you considered the start-up, operational, marketing costs etc. that will be required to maintain your side hustle monthly?

- Do you require a business partner, have you thought about the skills and the value that they can bring?

4

TIME MANAGEMENT FOR SIDE HUSTLERS

What's Time Got to Do With it?

Time is the most precious resource for a side hustler. Balancing your full-time job, personal life, and side hustle can be a juggling act. But with effective time management, you can make it work. In this chapter, we'll delve into the art of prioritizing your time, creating a side hustle schedule, and crucially, avoiding burnout, while remaining productive.

Identifying Your Most Productive Hours: Everyone has a time of day when they are most productive and alert. Some are early birds, while others are night owls. Identifying your peak productivity hours and scheduling your side hustle work during this time ensures that you make the most of your limited free time.

For example, if you're a morning person, you might find that your mind is sharpest before the world wakes up. This is an ideal time for focused work on your side hustle. On the other hand, if you're a night owl, late-night sessions might be when your creativity flows freely. Allocating your most challenging tasks to your peak hours can significantly increase your efficiency.

The Power of the 2-Hour Rule: Waiting for a large block of free time to tackle your side hustle is a common mistake. Life often doesn't offer such luxuries. Enter the "2-hour rule," a simple yet effective strategy: dedicate at least 2 hours each day to your side hustle, no matter what.

Even during your busiest days, finding 2 hours is manageable. It's like making a promise to yourself and your side hustle. Over a week, those 2-hour increments add up to a significant amount of focused work. This consistent effort keeps the momentum going and prevents procrastination from taking hold. If you are most productive early in the day, sending out all those emails or crossing out items on your task list between 6-8am, means you get to accomplish tasks for your side hustle, before the daily 9-5 grind takes over and demands your full attention.

The 80/20 Rule: The 80/20 rule, states that 80% of your results come from 20% of your efforts. Identifying the tasks that contribute the most to your side hustle's success and prioritizing them is crucial.

Rather than getting bogged down by small, low-impact tasks, focus on those that move the needle. Focus on the tasks that will really make a difference for your side hustle, for instance, if you're running an e-commerce side hustle, spending a significant portion of your time optimizing product listings, marketing strategies, or customer service can yield substantial results and drive-up sales.

It is important to note that the numbers don't have to be "80/20" exactly. The key point is that effort, reward, output are not distributed evenly, some contribute more than others, and you should understand where investing your time and efforts will yield the most effective results.

Creating A Side Hustle Schedule: A well-structured schedule can help you stay focused and committed to getting your tasks done and efficiently investing your time to get the most out of your tasks. Consistency is key, and a thoughtfully planned schedule can help you achieve it.

At the beginning of each week, take some time to create a detailed plan for your side hustle tasks. Set clear goals and deadlines for the week ahead. This not only keeps you organized but also helps you track your progress. As you complete each task, check it off your list to provide a sense of accomplishment and motivation.

Below is an example of a weekly schedule, but you can always adapt this to fit around your day job and your most productive hours.

Monday:

• 6:00 AM – 7:00 AM: Send order to suppliers and request quotes.

• 7:00 AM - 8:00 AM: Morning routine and preparation for the day job

• 9:00 AM - 5:30 PM: Full-time job

• 6:30 PM - 8:30 PM: Side hustle work - Content creation for social channels & Review supplier quotes and respond accordingly.

Tuesday:

• 6:00 AM – 7:00 AM: Schedule social media posts.

• 7:00 AM - 8:00 AM: Morning routine and preparation for the day job

• 9:00 AM - 5:30 PM: Full-time job

• 6:30 PM - 8:30 PM: Side hustle work (Product research and market analysis)

Wednesday:

• 6:00 AM – 7:00 AM: Place order with supplier.

• 7:00 AM - 8:00 AM: Morning routine and preparation for the day job

• 8:30 AM - 5:30 PM: Full-time job

• 6:30 PM - 8:30 PM: Side hustle work (Website maintenance and updates)

Thursday:

• 6:00 AM – 7:00 AM:

• 7:00 AM - 8:00 AM: Morning routine and preparation for the day job

• 8:30 AM - 5:30 PM: Full-time job

• 6:30 PM - 8:30 PM: Side hustle work (Customer outreach and marketing)

Friday:

• 7:00 AM - 8:00 AM: Morning routine and preparation for the day job

• 8:30 AM - 5:30 PM: Full-time job

• 6:30 PM - 8:30 PM: Side hustle work (Social media engagement and content scheduling)

Saturday:

• 9:00 AM - 11:00 AM: Side hustle work (Strategic planning and goal setting)

• 11:30 AM - 12:30 PM: Exercise and self-care

• 1:30 PM - 4:30 PM: Side hustle work (Meet with business partner to review tasks and business performance)

Sunday:

• 9:00 AM - 11:00 AM: Side hustle work (Me time,)

• 11:30 AM - 12:30 PM: Exercise and self-care

• 1:30 PM - 3:30 PM: Side hustle work (Financial planning and budgeting)

This schedule balances the demands of a full-time job with dedicated time for the side hustle. It allows for daily engagement with the side hustle in the evenings after work, with more extended blocks of time set aside on the weekends for tasks that require deeper focus.

Remember that your weekly schedule should be tailored to your specific circumstances, job hours, and side hustle goals. Flexibility is key, and adjustments may be necessary based on your progress and changing priorities.

In the digital age, various tools and apps, such as digital calendars, task and project management apps can assist you in managing your time effectively. These technologies can help you stay organized, automate repetitive tasks, track your progress, and help you to avoid being overwhelmed and burning out.

Avoiding Burnout and Mental Injury

While pursuing a side hustle is exciting, it's also crucial to avoid burnout. Burnout can happen when you're juggling multiple responsibilities and pushing yourself too hard. I see burnout as a mental injury, like an athlete who has developed an injury from overdoing it and can no longer perform and may even have to stop altogether until they recover. Burnout will impact your productivity negatively and therefore your side hustle. So, it's best to avoid burnout in the first place, and make sure that you aren't overdoing it. Here are strategies to prevent burnout:

Set Boundaries: It's easy to let your side hustle spill over into your personal life, especially when you're passionate about it. However, it's essential to set boundaries. Designate specific work hours for your side hustle, and when those hours are over, switch off and focus on personal time. Using a clearly defined weekly schedule should help you stay on top of this.

Self-Care is Non-Negotiable: Taking care of your physical and mental health is paramount. Make time for self-care activities, whether it's exercise, meditation, reading, or spending quality time with loved ones. Remember that you're in this for the long haul, and maintaining your well-being is key to long-term success.

Be Lazy, Learn to Delegate: If your side hustle reaches a point where you can't handle everything on your own, consider delegating tasks or seeking help. Whether it's hiring freelancers, partnering with others, or outsourcing specific functions, delegation can relieve some of the pressure.

Also consider tasks that you can be lazy about, where you don't have to be actively involved, but oversee the tasks and quality control. For example, if you have an online business or launching a new product, spending time learning to become a web developer or manufacturing the product by hand can put a lot of strain, stress, and consume brain power that you can use elsewhere where it makes a difference. Hire a website developer or outsource the manufacturing to avoid a steep learning curve, trial and error, etc.

Regularly Assess Your Workload: Periodically assess your workload and commitments. Are you taking on too much? Are there tasks that can be streamlined or eliminated? Adjust your schedule and responsibilities as needed to prevent overexertion.

The Ritual of Celebrating Small Wins: This is so important! Acknowledge and celebrate your achievements, no matter how small they may seem. Recognizing your progress boosts motivation and morale. It's a reminder that your hard work is paying off.

I used to work with an attitude where I never recognized my small wins, as I was waiting for those big wins and eventually, I felt like I failed when I didn't reach the big win. But with a change of mindset, I started to pay attention to the small wins and even came up with a ritual to celebrate quietly.

I would smoke a cigar and sip quietly on some rum and reflect on what I had achieved as a pat on the back; this helped boost my morale for the next milestone. Find a ritual that acts as a reward for yourself for the small win you have achieved, maybe a spa day, a weekend away, or a dinner with friends. Find what works for you and make it your ritual.

Conclusion

Time management is the linchpin of successful side hustling. By prioritizing your time, creating a well-structured schedule, and taking steps to prevent burnout, you can navigate the demands of your full-time job and side hustle with finesse. Remember, it's not about working more; it's about working smarter and more efficiently.

In the next chapter, we'll explore the importance of building and marketing your brand to get visibility in your marketplace.

Reflections

- When is your most productive time to work on your side hustle? Are you an early bird or a night owl?

- Can you dedicate at least 2 hours a day to your side hustle or build a detailed weekly schedule to stay on track?

- What tasks will really move the needle for your side hustle, and how will you focus on these?

- Consider how you will avoid burnout. What tasks can you delegate or outsource? How will you maintain your well-being? What is your ritual for celebrating small wins?

5

BRANDING & MARKETING ARE YOUR FRIENDS

What Are Branding and Marketing and Why Do You Need Them?

Establishing a strong brand is crucial for the growth of your side hustle. Your brand goes beyond a logo—it's the identity and values your business stands for. A well-defined brand helps build trust with your audience and sets you apart from the competition.

Equally important is marketing your brand effectively. Marketing allows you to communicate your brand's message, showcase your unique offerings, and connect with potential customers. Whether through social media, content marketing, or partnerships, a smart marketing strategy ensures your business stays visible and relevant.

Even with a limited budget, leveraging creative, low-cost tactics like social media marketing, email campaigns, and community engagement can help you reach a broader audience and turn your side hustle into a sustainable venture. Without marketing, even the best ideas struggle to gain traction, making it essential to invest time and resources into sharing your brand's story with the world. So, as we dive into this chapter, let's look at how you can create a brand that's not just memorable but also tells a story, and will make your side hustle stand out in the crowd by crafting a brand that speaks volumes in simple yet powerful ways.

Brand Values: Brand values are the fundamental principles and beliefs that form the bedrock of your business identity. They go beyond products or services, representing the intrinsic qualities that guide your business decisions and interactions. These values shape your business culture, influence customer perceptions, and define what your brand stands for.

Brand values provide continuity. While business strategies may evolve, core values remain relatively constant, creating a consistent identity over time. In essence, brand values are the soul of your business. They're not just a statement on a website; they're the lived experience of your brand, shaping how you operate and how you're perceived in the eyes of your audience. Think about what your values are and how you want them to resonate with your customers and audience and then shape your brand around these values.

Crafting a Unique Brand Proposition: What makes your side hustle stand out in a sea of competition? Enter your Unique Selling Proposition (USP), the secret sauce that distinguishes your brand. Essentially you want to make your side hustle unique, something that isn’t readily available in the marketplace or that your competitors currently don’t offer but there is a demand for. Whether it's a ground-breaking product, outstanding service, or an innovative concept, defining precisely what makes your side hustle unique forms the cornerstone of your brand identity. Your USP becomes the narrative that captures attention and fosters loyalty among your audience.

For example, if you are a graphic designer that helps businesses with their brand identity and logo designs, you can offer a USP that you can deliver their "business logo in 1 hour". The combination of speed of delivery and good quality work can then be your USP, which could be hard for competitors to beat and will get the attention of your customers.

Designing a Striking Visual Identity: Your visual identity is a powerful tool for brand communication. It helps in creating a memorable and distinctive brand image, fostering recognition, and influencing how the audience perceives the brand's personality and values. A visual identity isn't necessary for your side hustle, but it will help you stand out or be easily recognizable with your customers, especially if you aim to have a long-term side hustle.

Your brand's visual identity is the collection of visual elements that uniquely and cohesively represent a brand. It goes beyond just a logo; it encompasses various design elements and style choices that create a consistent and recognizable look for the brand, such as colors, typography, photography, imagery and even tone of voice.

These visual elements play a crucial role in shaping how the brand is perceived by its audience.

Marketing Your Side Business on a Limited Budget

In the world of side hustles and business in general, marketing is a crucial part of your business and hustle plan, a lot of small businesses and side hustles neglect to include marketing spends or budgets in their plans when they launch, this is a mistake! Marketing not only gets your hustle noticed and builds an awareness of your service with the audience, but it can also build relationships, connections and loyalty with your audience that can lead to revenue generation.

Think of your marketing strategy as your first salesperson, who reaches your audience where they are, on their phone, screen etc. Your marketing strategy doesn't have to break the bank, of course, the more you invest into marketing the more you get out of it, but with the onset of marketing channels like social media you can start with a few hundred dollars.

However, it is important that you stay consistent and always on so that you remain consistent and top of mind with your audience.

Below are some marketing tactics you can incorporate into your strategy:

Guerrilla Marketing Tactics: Think outside the conventional marketing box. Guerrilla marketing involves unconventional and imaginative strategies to capture attention. It could be eye-catching street art, impromptu flash mobs, or inventive social media campaigns. The essence lies in generating significant buzz without a substantial financial investment. These tactics are about creating memorable experiences that stick in the minds of your audience, fostering a connection that traditional methods might miss.

Content Marketing on a Shoestring Budget: Quality content stands out as a formidable weapon in your marketing arsenal. Crafting engaging and valuable content tailored to your audience can be a compelling strategy. Blog posts, videos, or infographics not only showcase your expertise but also act as magnets, drawing individuals toward your side hustle. Explore the plethora of free or low-cost platforms to host your content and share it across social media channels. Consistent, valuable content builds credibility and keeps your audience engaged.

Collaborations and Partnerships: Building a network of collaborations and partnerships can greatly expand your reach. Start by identifying individuals or businesses that align with your brand's values and goals. This could involve co-hosting events, participating in cross-promotions, or partnering with influencers. These collaborations offer an effective way to grow without significant financial investment. By leveraging each other's audiences, resources, and strengths, you can create mutually beneficial relationships that help both parties succeed.

Speaking opportunities & Networking: Speaking opportunities and networking at events and conferences provide an opportunity to present your side hustle to an engaged audience, although on a smaller scale compared to online mass marketing, it gives you the opportunity to present you services/products in an in-depth way that can attract new business.

Consider creating a presentation that showcases your offering, the benefits of working with you and customer testimonials.

Leveraging social media and Online Presence: Online and social media marketing is integral to you marketing plans, if you're not online you aren't in business or finding growth for your side hustle will be challenging without an online presence. Starting your social media and online marketing is quite accessible and cost effective nowadays compared to say a TV or Radio commercial, which demand significant costs. And most social and online channels cater for SMEs and start-ups with a self-serve approach allowing you to be targeted in who you want to reach, so there isn't really an excuse for not getting involved.

Influencer Marketing: You don't have to spend exorbitant amount of money to get an influencer to showcase your products or services, consider working with micro influencers who have a few hundred or a few thousand followers. Some micro influencers can even showcase your business in a barter deal for an exchange of your products or services for theirs. This is a cost-effective way to get them to become brand ambassadors for your business and reach an audience that already trusts and listens to the influencer.

However, it's important to ensure you match the right influencer, for example if you have a sustainable fashion brand then, influencers who champion sustainability within the fashion industry will be a good match.

Optimizing Your Website for Conversions: Your website is often the initial point of contact with potential customers, playing a pivotal role in shaping their perception of your brand. Ensure it's not just visually appealing but also user-friendly, steering visitors seamlessly toward conversions. From compelling product descriptions to a streamlined checkout process or contact number or form. Every element should be designed to guide visitors toward making a purchase or engaging with your services. The goal is to make the customer journey smooth and enjoyable, converting visitors into loyal customers.

Use Search Engine Marketing to make your website visible and rank highly on search engines, so customers can easily search and find your website. Use free tools such as Google Analytics and Social Media Pixels to gain insights into who visits your websites and the actions, they take on the site.

Email Marketing for Customer Retention: Establishing and nurturing customer relationships takes center stage through email marketing. Cultivate a mailing list and initiate regular communication, be it updates, exclusive offers, or informative newsletters. Email marketing stands out as a cost-effective avenue for retaining customers and fostering repeat business. By providing valuable content directly to your customers' inboxes, you stay top of mind, increasing the likelihood that they'll turn to your side hustle when in need of relevant products or services.

Free email marketing tools such as MailChimp, HubSpot and Sender can be used to run your email campaigns, while keeping your costs down.

Conclusion

Building your brand on some level is important to the creation of your side hustle, it's how you determine what's important to you, what you stand for and what differentiates you from the competition.

Creating your brand allows you to communicate easily and consistently what your side hustle is all about to your audience in a way that resonates with them and encourages them to do business with you. Your marketing strategy will help bring visibility and new business for you, and by employing cost-effective channels such as a website and social media marketing you will be able reach new audiences and drive growth and engagement for your side hustle.

Reflections

• How can you clearly articulate your brand values, USP and Messaging?

• Have you considered your brand and visual identity, what do you want your target audience to think and feel when they see your brand?

• What marketing strategy or channels will work best for your side hustle and will resonate with your audience?

• Have you considered a monthly marketing budget?

6

LAUNCHING YOUR SIDE HUSTLE

Ready, Set, Side Hustle: Will Your Idea Take Off?

Embarking on your entrepreneurial journey, especially with the launch of your side hustle, marks a significant achievement. It's the culmination of your vision, hard work, and meticulous planning. This chapter will delve into the crucial aspects of kickstarting your side hustle journey, ensuring a strategic approach for sustained success and growth. We'll explore the nuances of testing the waters, gradually scaling up, and learning from the inevitable challenges. This phase is where your side hustle evolves from a mere concept into a tangible reality, propelling you toward fulfilment and success with purposeful strides.

The Soft Launch: Testing the Waters

Starting your own business is a big deal and launching your side hustle is a crucial step in that journey. Before diving in fully, it's smart to do a soft launch—a sort of trial run where you can test things out, and fix any issues before going all in. It's like dipping your toes in the water to see how it feels before taking the plunge. This helps ensure a smoother journey ahead. Below are some of the ways a soft lunch can benefit your side hustle.

Gathering Feedback: A limited audience will allow you for focused feedback, unveiling nuanced insights into customer preferences, pain points, and areas for improvement. By actively seeking opinions, you can decipher what resonates with your audience and refine your offering accordingly.

Identifying Issues: Acting as a trial run, a soft launch brings potential challenges to the forefront, ranging from technical glitches to customer queries. Proactively addressing these issues ensures a polished and seamless experience when your side hustle reaches a broader audience.

Building Buzz: A soft launch isn't merely a behind-the-scenes operation; it's an exclusive preview that generates anticipation and curiosity among your target audience. This initial buzz can translate into a heightened interest that paves the way for a more impactful grand launch.

Adapt and Refine Before Going All Out

Based on the feedback received, embark on a dynamic process of adaptation and refinement.

Iteratively refine your products, services, or processes, ensuring they align with the expectations and preferences of your audience.

In essence, the soft launch serves as a strategic compass, guiding you through the early stages of your side hustle. It's a methodical approach to unveil insights, correct course, and set the stage for a more impactful and successful full-scale launch. By understanding the nuances of your audience's response and continuously adapting, you position your side hustle for resilience and long-term growth in the competitive entrepreneurial landscape.

For example, if you are launching a clothing brand, you can start with a soft launch and test the market by taking pre-orders of your garments from customers, this will allow you to get feedback on things such as, are they happy with the price range, quality of clothing and customer service. You can then take this feedback and apply to the main to the main launch.

Scaling Your Side Business Gradually

Scaling your side business is a marathon, not a sprint. Gradual growth ensures sustainability and maintains the quality that attracted your initial customers. It's a deliberate and strategic process.

While sprinting might give the illusion of speed, a marathon approach emphasizes endurance and longevity. Similarly, gradual scaling is about enduring success, maintaining quality, and strategically advancing at a pace that aligns with your business's capacity.

One of the key reasons to opt for gradual scaling is to uphold the quality that drew your initial customers. Rapid expansion can strain resources and, in the haste to grow, compromise the very essence that made your business attractive. By scaling gradually, you ensure that each step forward is accompanied by the necessary support and resources to sustain, or even enhance, the quality your customers appreciate.

Stress Testing for Operational Resilience: Think of gradual scaling as stress testing your business operations. It's a methodical approach to identify and address potential bottlenecks before they transform into critical issues. By taking measured steps, you can refine and streamline your processes, ensuring that your business operations are resilient and capable of handling increased demands.

Nurturing Customer Relationships: The beauty of gradual growth lies in its ability to allow you to adapt and nurture individual customer relationships. Rapid expansion often makes it challenging to provide a personalized experience, as the focus shifts to quantity over quality. With gradual scaling, you can cultivate strong connections with your customers, understanding their evolving needs and preferences as you grow together.

Evaluate Demand with Precision: Before taking steps to scale, carefully evaluate the demand for your products or services. Incremental scaling should be a response to demonstrated increases in customer interest. This involves analyzing customer feedback, monitoring sales trends, and gauging the market to ensure that your business is ready for expansion.

Expand Thoughtfully with New Offerings: Gradual scaling isn't just about doing more of the same; it's about doing more strategically. Introduce new products or services based on a deep understanding of customer needs. This not only attracts a wider audience but also keeps existing customers engaged and excited about what your side business has to offer.

Invest in a Solid Infrastructure: As you scale, your business infrastructure must evolve in tandem. This includes technology, production capacity, and customer support. Invest in systems and processes that can handle gradual increases in demand without compromising efficiency or customer satisfaction. A solid foundation ensures that your business can thrive as it expands.

Monitor Key Metrics Religiously: Keep a close eye on key performance indicators (KPIs) to gauge the health of your business. Metrics such as customer acquisition cost, customer lifetime value, and conversion rates provide invaluable insights into the effectiveness of your scaling efforts. Regular monitoring allows you to make informed decisions and course corrections as needed.

Learning from Initial Challenges: Challenges in the initial phase are opportunities for growth, not roadblocks. Embrace them, learn from them, and use them to fortify your entrepreneurial journey.

Reflections

• What aspects of your side hustle could benefit from a soft launch? How can you implement a limited release to gather valuable feedback?

• In what ways can you apply the marathon mindset to your side hustle's growth? How does gradual scaling align with your long-term goals?

- Which areas of your side hustle can benefit from incremental scaling, and how can you strategically introduce new offerings to enhance customer engagement and sales?

- What challenges do you foresee in your side hustle and how will embrace and overcome them?

7

MANAGING YOUR FINANCES

Making Cents of Your Future

You've done all the due diligence and launched your side hustle, you're making sales, and the hustle is relatively paying off, but how should you manage your revenue and spending to keep your hustle successful and sustainable.

Managing the finances and revenue of a side hustle is crucial for its long-term success and sustainability. Proper financial management allows entrepreneurs to track income and expenses, ensuring that they can identify profitable areas and address any financial challenges promptly. By keeping detailed records, side hustlers can make informed decisions about reinvesting profits, scaling operations, or even pivoting their business model if necessary. Additionally, sound financial practices help in budgeting for taxes and planning for unexpected expenses, which can mitigate risks and enhance overall stability. Ultimately, effective financial management not only contributes to a side hustle's growth but also fosters a sense of accountability and professionalism, paving the way for potential future ventures.

Managing Side Hustle Income

As you embark on your side hustle journey, effectively managing your income will be a critical skill. Let's explore the intricacies of handling your side hustle earnings together. This includes setting up a dedicated business account, implementing efficient invoicing practices, budgeting for stability, allocating funds for emergencies, developing reinvestment strategies, diversifying income streams, and practicing prudent debt management.

Establish a Dedicated Business Account: Managing your side hustle income begins with creating a clear demarcation between personal and business finances. Open a separate business bank account to streamline financial tracking, manage expenses efficiently, and facilitate transparent record-keeping.

Implement Robust Invoicing Practices: Now, let's talk about invoicing. Timely and accurate invoices are crucial for maintaining a healthy cash flow. Utilize professional invoicing tools or templates to clearly outline services or products provided, payment terms, and due dates.

Budgeting for Stability: As your side hustle income grows, effective budgeting becomes essential. Develop a comprehensive budget that encompasses both operational and growth-oriented expenses. Allocate funds judiciously, ensuring that essential aspects such as marketing, technology, and personnel are adequately funded.

Emergency Fund Allocation: Set aside a portion of your income into an emergency fund. This financial buffer serves as a safety net during lean periods or unexpected expenses, fostering stability and resilience.

Reinvestment Strategies: Strategically reinvest a portion of your profits back into your side hustle. Whether it's upgrading equipment, expanding your product line, or investing in professional development, reinvestment fuels long-term growth.

Diversify Income Streams: Explore avenues for diversifying your income streams within the realm of your side hustle. This not only safeguards against overreliance on a single source but also positions your venture for adaptability in fluctuating market conditions.

Debt Management: Exercise prudence in managing debt. While judicious borrowing for strategic growth is acceptable, avoid accumulating unnecessary debt that could strain your financial stability. Priorities paying off high-interest debts promptly.

Tax Considerations for Side Hustlers

Managing taxes is essential for side hustlers for several key reasons. First, staying on top of tax obligations helps avoid late fees and penalties, which can accumulate quickly if overlooked. Additionally, proper tax management allows side hustlers to maximize deductions, reducing taxable income and ultimately lowering tax liabilities.

Understanding tax obligations also enables better financial planning and budgeting, ensuring that sufficient funds are set aside for tax payments. Furthermore, knowing that taxes are managed properly provides peace of mind, allowing side hustlers to focus on growing their business rather than worrying about potential tax issues.

Let's explore the details together, ensuring you're fully prepared to navigate the tax landscape with confidence. We'll discuss the importance of separating personal and business expenses, staying informed about your tax obligations, maintaining accurate records, identifying key deductions, making quarterly estimated tax payments, and the benefits of seeking professional tax assistance.

Separate Personal and Business Expenses: First things first, ensure a clear distinction between your personal and business expenses. This not only makes bookkeeping simpler but is a crucial step for accurate tax reporting. Avoid commingling funds to save yourself from unnecessary complexities during tax season.

Stay Informed on Tax Obligations: Tax obligations can vary based on your business structure and location. Stay informed about the specific requirements in your jurisdiction. Regularly review tax codes and consider seeking professional advice to ensure compliance. Being proactive in understanding your obligations is key.

Record-Keeping Excellence: Meticulous record-keeping is your best friend during tax season. Keep detailed records of all financial transactions, including income, expenses, receipts, and invoices. Consider using digital accounting tools or professional services to streamline this process, making tax preparation less stressful.

Understand Deductions Available: Familiarize yourself with potential tax deductions for your side hustle. This could include deductions for home office costs, equipment purchases, professional development expenses, and even a portion of your utility bills. Knowing and maximizing these deductions can significantly optimize your tax position.

Quarterly Estimated Tax Payments: Unlike traditional employment, side hustlers often don't have taxes automatically withheld from their income. To avoid a substantial tax bill at the end of the fiscal year, take a proactive approach. Calculate and make quarterly estimated tax payments. This ensures financial preparedness and minimizes the risk of penalties.

Professional Tax Assistance:

Consider enlisting the services of a tax professional or utilizing reliable accounting software for comprehensive tax assistance. Professional guidance can uncover potential deductions, ensure accurate filings, and provide strategic advice for optimizing your tax position. It's an investment that pays off in peace of mind and potentially significant savings.

Conclusion

Navigating the tax landscape might seem daunting, but with these practical steps, you're well on your way to ensuring a smooth and compliant journey. Remember, staying organized, informed, and seeking professional assistance when needed are the keys to mastering your side hustle taxes.

So, there you have it—managing your side hustle income is a delicate balancing act. We've covered the basics from separating personal and business finances to strategic reinvestment. It's about ensuring stability, fostering growth, and steering your side hustle towards lasting success.

Reflections

- How can you refine your budget to align more closely with your side hustle's growth trajectory?

- Contemplate your long-term financial goals for your side hustle. How do these goals align with your personal aspirations and the evolving landscape of your industry?

- Are you finding the right balance between reinvesting in your side hustle's growth and generating profits?

- How robust are your contingency plans, and how effectively do they address potential challenges?

8

NAVIGATING CHALLENGES

How Do Side Hustlers Stay Afloat While Juggling It All?

The journey of entrepreneurship, whether through a side hustle or a startup, is both challenging and rewarding. Overcoming obstacles not only leads to success but also fosters resilience and perseverance. Challenges drive personal and professional growth, with hurdles like uncertainty and stress pushing individuals to develop their skills.

While fear of failure can hold aspiring entrepreneurs back, taking small steps—such as freelancing or seeking feedback—can ignite their journey. Instead of viewing ambiguity and stress as setbacks, entrepreneurs can see them as opportunities to boost productivity. Without a steady income, they must rely on their ability to adapt.

Identity crises are common, as personal and professional lives often blur. Maintaining balance is vital to prevent burnout and mental health issues. Financial concerns can be daunting for those starting from necessity, but careful planning can turn these challenges into opportunities for financial expertise.

Overcoming Common Side Hustle Challenges

As startups grow, they encounter intense competition, high expectations, and recruitment challenges. Resilience and perseverance are crucial to navigate these obstacles. Setbacks should be viewed as learning opportunities, with successful entrepreneurs embracing challenges and continuously moving forward. Ultimately, the entrepreneurial journey transforms individuals into resilient leaders capable of thriving in an ever-changing landscape. Below we can look at some pointers to guide you through challenges you might face.

Simply Starting the Work: The initial step into entrepreneurship is akin to standing at the edge of the unknown. The comfort of routine often deters us from taking the plunge into the unpredictable realm of a side hustle or freelancing. The fear of rejection, failure and concerns about the investment of time and money can be paralyzing. They key is to just get started and put your fears to the side, remember, the journey of a thousand miles begins with a single step. By initiating small projects and seeking feedback, you gradually build the confidence and momentum needed for more significant undertakings.

Work with Mentors: Mentors play a crucial role in guiding and supporting entrepreneurs as they build their side hustles. Having a mentor provides invaluable insights, advice, and perspective gained from their own experiences. Mentors can offer practical guidance on navigating challenges, making strategic decisions, and avoiding common pitfalls.

They also serve as a sounding board for ideas, helping entrepreneurs refine their vision and strategies. Mentors often have extensive networks that they can tap into, providing valuable connections and opportunities for collaboration or partnerships. Additionally, mentors can offer emotional support, encouragement, and motivation during the ups and downs of entrepreneurship.

Overall, having a mentor can significantly accelerate the growth and success of a side hustle by providing guidance, expertise, and support along the way.

Build a Business Network: By expanding your network, you can access new markets, partnerships, and referrals, which can lead to increased visibility and growth for their business. Additionally, being part of a network provides a sense of community and support, helping you gain support and shared knowledge from others who are going through as similar journey.

<u>Stress and Instability</u>

The entrepreneurial journey, especially in a side hustle, introduces a level of stress and instability not encountered in traditional employment. The unpredictability of the market directly impacts your workload, and unlike a salaried job, there's no guaranteed fallback work during lean periods. To counteract stress and maintain stability, consider the following tactics:

Emphasize Productivity: In the face of uncertainty, productivity becomes your guiding light. Establish a routine that emphasizes efficiency and time management. This not only enhances your output but also provides a sense of control amid market fluctuations.

Diversify Income Streams: Explore avenues to diversify your income within the realm of your side hustle. Having multiple revenue streams not only safeguards against overreliance on a single source but also provides stability in fluctuating market conditions.

Navigating stress and instability requires a proactive approach. By fostering a productive mindset and diversifying your income streams, you can build a resilient foundation for your side hustle.

Identity Crisis

The pursuit of high productivity can inadvertently lead to an identity crisis. As your work becomes intricately linked with your identity, setbacks in your professional life may translate to personal failures. Maintaining a clear separation between your professional and personal life is crucial for long-term well-being. Here's how:

Establish Boundaries: Define clear boundaries between work and personal life. Designate specific working hours and create a dedicated workspace. This demarcation helps prevent work from permeating every aspect of your existence.

Cultivate Hobbies and Interests: Outside of your professional endeavors, cultivate hobbies and interests that are unrelated to your side hustle. This diversification provides a mental break and contributes to a more balanced, fulfilling life.

Remember, your identity extends beyond your professional achievements. By consciously establishing boundaries and nurturing personal interests, you safeguard your mental and emotional well-being.

Embrace Failure

When setbacks occur, it's important to avoid fixating on disappointment or assigning blame to yourself. Instead, reframe setbacks as valuable learning opportunities that provide insight into your journey. Take the time to deconstruct the root cause of the setback, analyzing what went wrong and why. This reflective process can reveal key areas for improvement, whether in your approach to decision-making, communication, or teamwork.

Embrace candid self-assessment, recognizing that acknowledging your weaknesses is a critical step toward personal growth.

Engaging in constructive self-reflection also opens the door to seeking feedback from peers or mentors. This collaborative approach can provide new perspectives and ideas on how to navigate challenges more effectively. Remember, personal development is an ongoing journey; each setback is not a failure but a steppingstone toward becoming a more resilient and capable entrepreneur. By cultivating a growth mindset, you empower yourself to learn from every experience, adapt to challenges, and ultimately thrive in your entrepreneurial endeavors.

Reflections

- Reflect on your hesitation to start. What small steps can you take today to test your entrepreneurial aspirations?

- Reflect on your coping mechanisms for stress. Are there adjustments you can make to enhance your emotional well-being?

- Explore the link between productivity and personal identity. In what ways can you consciously separate work and personal life?

- Consider your adaptability. In what ways can you cultivate a mindset that embraces failure, change and learning?

9

NETWORKING AND SUPPORT

Are You Ready to Be Connected?

Running a side hustle can be emotionally taxing, especially when faced with obstacles and setbacks. A supportive community offers a safe space to share struggles, vent frustrations, and seek encouragement from others who understand the entrepreneurial journey.

Building a support community is not just important for the success of a side hustler's business; it's essential for their overall well-being. Entrepreneurship can be a lonely and challenging journey, filled with uncertainty, setbacks, and moments of self-doubt. Having a support system in place provides emotional encouragement, practical advice, and a sense of camaraderie that can make all the difference.

The solitary journey of a side hustler is often illuminated by the connections they forge and the support they garner from a robust network. This chapter delves into the profound impact of networking, the role of mentors, and the significance of a support structure to nurture and sustain your entrepreneurial spirit.

Building a Supportive Network

Building a strong business network is crucial for driving your venture forward. Networking goes beyond merely exchanging business cards; it involves forming connections based on shared experiences and mutual support during the ups and downs of entrepreneurship.

Consider the power of these connections: they can lead to collaborations with individuals who share your passion and vision. Networking isn't just about what you can gain; it's equally about what you can contribute. By fostering meaningful relationships rather than just collecting contacts, you create a vibrant community that benefits everyone involved.

Collaboration plays a key role in entrepreneurship, as working together on projects or sharing resources can enhance growth for all parties. In a crowded marketplace, trust becomes invaluable; genuine connections build credibility and unlock new opportunities.

Think of networking as tending to a garden—it requires time and effort, but the rewards are well worth it. By nurturing these relationships, you cultivate a supportive community where everyone can thrive, ensuring your side hustle not only survives but flourishes.

Practical Advice and Guidance: Mentors and peers within a support network can offer valuable insights, guidance, and feedback based on their own experiences. Whether it's navigating business challenges, making important decisions, or learning new skills, having access to diverse perspectives can help side hustlers make informed choices and avoid common pitfalls.

Motivation and Accountability: Building a support community provides side hustlers with a network of accountability partners who can help them stay focused, motivated, and accountable to their goals. Knowing that others are cheering them on and holding them to their commitments can boost motivation and productivity.

Resilience and Mental Health: A supportive community can serve as a buffer against stress and anxiety, providing encouragement, empathy, and practical strategies for managing stress and maintaining well-being.

In essence, building a support community is not just about business success; it's about fostering a sense of belonging, resilience, and personal growth.

By surrounding yourself with a supportive network of mentors, peers, and like-minded individuals, you can navigate the ups and downs of entrepreneurship with greater confidence, resilience, and overall well-being.

Finding Mentors and Accountability Partners

In the previous chapter on "Navigating Challenges", we touched on the benefits and importance of working with mentors. They're like a trusted friend, offering advice and wisdom to help you navigate the ups and downs of entrepreneurship based on their experience and seasoned knowledge.

But how do you find a mentor and choose the right mentor?

Identify Your Needs: Think about what specific areas you need guidance in. Whether it's marketing, finance, or leadership, knowing your needs will help you find a mentor with the right expertise.

Tap Into Your Network: Reach out to your existing network – friends, colleagues, and industry contacts. They may know someone who would be a great mentor for you.

Attend Events and Workshops: Industry events and workshops are great places to meet potential mentors. Look for people who are knowledgeable and approachable.

Research Online: Use online platforms like LinkedIn to search for professionals in your industry who have the skills and experience you're looking for in a mentor. Reach out to them and explain what you are looking for, you will be surprised how many are willing to help.

Reach Out: Once you've identified potential mentors, don't be afraid to reach out to them. Send a polite and concise message explaining why you admire their work and how you think they could help you.

Assess Compatibility: When meeting potential mentors, pay attention to how well you click. It's important to have a good rapport and feel comfortable discussing your challenges and goals.

Establish Expectations: Be clear about your expectations and goals for the relationship. Agree on how often you'll meet and what topics you'll focus on.

Joining Online Communities

Joining online communities is a game-changer for modern entrepreneurs looking to expand their horizons in the digital world. These virtual spaces are more than just websites – they're bustling hubs of collaboration, inspiration, and encouragement, bringing together people from all walks of life and corners of the globe. By jumping into online communities that match their interests, entrepreneurs unlock a treasure trove of knowledge, experiences, and connections that can supercharge their businesses.

Picking the right online community is key for entrepreneurs aiming to make the most of virtual networking. Platforms tailored to their industry or passions provide a stage for sharing stories, seeking advice, and gaining valuable insights. By actively participating in these communities, entrepreneurs turn digital acquaintances into real relationships, building bonds and teamwork.

But online communities aren't just about business – they're about building a sense of belonging. Members cheer each other on, offer encouragement during tough times, and form bonds that extend beyond the digital realm. By diving into these communities, entrepreneurs build meaningful connections, gain fresh perspectives, and become part of a supportive network that fuels their growth and success.

In the entrepreneurial journey, online communities are invaluable. They're places to learn, connect, and find support. By joining the right ones, entrepreneurs can access a world of resources, connect with like-minded peers, and tap into a community that's there for them every step of the way.

Here are some examples of online and offline business communities where entrepreneurs can network, share knowledge, and collaborate:

- LinkedIn Groups
- Reddit
- Quora Spaces
- Startup Accelerator Communities
- Local Business Chambers
- Industry Conferences and Events
- Coworking Spaces
- Entrepreneurial Meetups
- Online Courses and Webinars

Conclusion

By actively engaging in networking activities, seeking mentorship, and building a strong support network, entrepreneurs can enhance their chances of success and navigate the challenges of entrepreneurship with confidence and resilience.

Reflections

- What attributes are you looking for in a mentor and what would you need from them?

- Can you identify anyone within your network that can be your accountability partner, and what areas do you want them to focus on?

- Are you part of an online or entrepreneurship community, if not what type of community will benefit your business needs and how can you contribute to these communities?

10

THE JOURNEY AHEAD

Is Your Map Set for Success?

As we reach the final chapter of our journey together, it's a good time to pause and reflect on the valuable insights you've gained throughout this book. From the beginning stages of your side hustle idea to the practical steps needed to make it a reality, we've covered a range of topics aimed at helping you start and sustain your side hustle with confidence. Each chapter has focused on providing you with straightforward strategies and tips to navigate the challenges and opportunities that come your way. My goal has been to equip you with the knowledge and tools you need to succeed in your side hustle journey.

We started by recognizing the benefits of engaging in a side hustle, acknowledging its potential to provide financial stability, personal fulfillment, and a pathway to achieving long-term goals. We discussed the delicate balance required when managing a full-time job alongside a burgeoning side business, emphasizing the importance of a job that is your business partner

Identify your passions and skills, recognize that the intersection of what you love and what you excel at holds the key to a fulfilling side hustle, if there is a demand in the market and low risk, refer to the "Side Hustle Formula".

With your idea in hand, we moved on to the crucial stage of planning. We emphasized the significance of understanding your target audience and crafting a solid business plan to guide your endeavors. Setting realistic expectations and budgeting for your side business were highlighted as essential components of this planning phase, ensuring that you embark on your journey with clarity and foresight.

Time management emerged as a recurring theme throughout our discussions, as we recognized the inherent challenge of balancing multiple responsibilities. We looked strategies for prioritizing tasks, creating a manageable schedule, and safeguarding against burnout, emphasizing the importance of self-care and maintaining a healthy work-life balance.

The launch of your side hustle marked a significant milestone in your journey. We looked at the importance of testing the waters with a soft launch, gradually scaling your business as you gain confidence and traction. We acknowledged the inevitable challenges that accompany this phase and emphasized the value of learning from setbacks and adapting your approach accordingly.

As your side hustle begins to generate income, we turned our attention to the practicalities of managing your finances. We explored strategies for effectively managing your side hustle income, navigating tax considerations, and planning for the future, ensuring that your business remains sustainable and profitable in the long run.

Challenges are an inevitable part of any entrepreneurial journey, and we dedicated a chapter to navigating them with resilience and perseverance. We looked at common challenges faced by side hustlers including stress, identity crisis and the big F, failure, and offered strategies for overcoming them, emphasizing the importance of building a supportive network and learning from both successes and setbacks and embracing failure.

Networking and support were identified as invaluable resources on your side hustle journey. We explored the process of building a supportive network, finding mentors and accountability partners, and engaging with online and offline communities to share knowledge and experiences.

Encouragement to Start Your Side Hustle

As you take a moment to reflect on the wealth of insights gathered from each chapter of this book, I urge you to approach your side hustle journey with a sense of confidence and unwavering determination. It's crucial to recognize that while the path ahead may be strewn with challenges and uncertainties, each obstacle presents a unique opportunity for personal growth and invaluable learning experiences.

The prospect of starting a side hustle might initially seem daunting, perhaps even overwhelming. However, it's essential to remember that every successful venture begins with that crucial first step, no matter how small it may appear.

Embrace the journey wholeheartedly, trusting in your abilities and staying true to the passions that have ignited your entrepreneurial spirit.

Equip yourself with the knowledge and tools acquired throughout the pages of this book and come back to it whenever you need it and let this book serve as your guiding compass as you embark on this exciting endeavor. Now is the time to translate theory into action, to turn your dreams into tangible realities. Believe in yourself, for you possess the resilience and determination needed to navigate the challenges that lie ahead.

Here's to your success, both in business and in life. May your journey be filled with endless possibilities and abundant fulfillment.

Remember, you are not alone on this journey, you can watch and hear from other entrepreneurs about their challenges, failures and success in business or side hustle, all on my podcast - Real People Real Business.

Scan The Code to Watch and Subscribe!

www.ingramcontent.com/pod-product-compliance
Lightning Source LLC
LaVergne TN
LVHW010500160826
845677LV00012B/2572
* 9 7 8 9 3 5 8 4 7 5 1 7 3 *